United In Freedom

An epic poem

By

Meryl M Williams

The Poet Meryl M Williams b1966

Meryl was born in the heart of the South Wales coal fields with Cwm Colliery in the neighbourhood of her first home. She is a qualified scientist, having worked in London, Bath and Texas, USA before settling in Bath to write first poetry then prose.

Meryl enjoys walks in the countryside and takes all her own photographs.

This book is dedicated to her former support manager and his able team, for making the work possible. Meryl would also like to thank the Wilberforce House Museum and the M Shed Museum for invaluable information and insight.

Copyright © 2026 Meryl M Williams
ISBN: 978-1-918424-29-4

Author's Note

In the preparation of this, my second epic poem, I was reminded of a very talented creative writing tutor and his pertinent wisdom. He said,
"Don't put your full English breakfast, your roast dinner and your sponge pudding all on the same plate".

In many respects this is what I've done. To put together a picture of life at the early part of the 19th Century when the Slavery Abolition Act was passed, I have included many things that were being discovered at that time. We read of new products from the Industrial Revolution such as gas street lamps, steam railway engines and photography but in addition, we also read of big changes in social awareness such as the introduction of votes for women at the beginning of the 20th Century.

Finally, we read how struggles for peace in conflict zones, and the call for equal opportunity with freedom across the Globe is still an ongoing movement.

CONTENTS

UNITED IN FREEDOM

Part 1   A European Demand.   Page 6

Part 2. Seeds of Change.   14

Part 3. Thank you, Mr Speaker.   27

Part 4. Vision and More.   33

Part 5. A Constant Battle.   36

Home Loving Rhymes.   39

Plate 1. Wilberforce House Museum, Kingston Upon Hull, Yorkshire, UK.

UNITED IN FREEDOM

Part One.   A European Demand.

Man's inhumanity to man
Returns as War and strife,
Yet oft' a quiet revolution
Is all we can achieve this life.

Here was a man, a good MP
Born in comfort to trade,
Now remembered throughout History
For a change so timely made.

We will see, as the tale unfolds,
That this revolution one man upheld.
That continues right up to today,
With protests needed and overdue apologies made.

We'll read of men who raided Earth
Trading in humans like their herds,
Disregarding mortal flesh as frail, as if
They had superiority in their supremacy.

Yes money may buy goods or land

But never prevents death's grip or hand,
We cannot escape our mortal fate
Then the Day of Judgment is a day too late.

Four hundred years of torture
Cruelty to enslaved people
Death to many, wealth to some
Ended by an Act of Parliament
Brought about by one white man.

But others sought abolition, to include
A familiar name; the Poet and painter
William Blake famous for "Tyger, Tyger"
And the rousing words to "Jerusalem".

Other people took the lead
To boycott sugar, women held
The choice of purchase for the home
So took the profit from this abhorrent trade.

The City of Bristol had busy docks
Which just for a Century shipped
Enslaved people from the Americas
The Caribbean, trading humankind
For shoddy goods.

If you look across the Bay
This is how it looks today,
Would you believe from this tranquil scene
The torment that took place in yesteryear?

See in the image the tracks for cranes,
Used to load cargo such as timber logs
All out of use now just a pleasure trip
Upon a replica tall ship.

Plate 2. Bristol docks from the first floor of the M Shed Museum.

Transatlantic traffic of enslaved people
Began in Europe at the latter part
Of the fifteenth Century, then sugar
Consumption doubled in Britain across
The turn of the eighteenth. It gives
An indication of the scale of the traffic,
Four centuries of horror and for just
One hundred years of this, the docks
Of Bristol played it's part.

Rich and powerful plantation owners
Owned slaves that had been forced
To work cotton fields, plus tobacco
As well as sugar cane and beet.

But as if to offset a life of guilt
Good works were considered
Philanthropy, helping the poor
Or charitable aims, but only where
White boys were concerned.

Shackles were a particular abomination
Used to control enslaved people,
With force, a weight of iron
A chain of metal
A hangover from Medieval times

Surviving to this day as handcuffs
The humiliation of such treatment
No words will ever describe.

Their use is not continued
Around the ankle, I admit,
But with your wrists in bondage,
Powerless is how I would define
The experience of large, burly men
Towering over me, yanking my arms
While all I could do was submit.

How they sleep at night, I'll never know
While the squirrel races up the fence
Finding a gap in the barbed wire,
Left there I presume for
The sniffer dogs to go.

But my acquiescence was dearly bought
With the over tranquilising use of a nasty drug,
So many women I'm sad to say
Were given diazapan to be out of the way.

I'd only taken it once before
It's use is wrong, but men use force,
I had to take my usual prescription

This drug was introduced then I refused
But by then it was too late, they had locked the door.

So much for authority
As likely as us all,
To bask in glorious sunshine
While the Poet Blake reminds me
Of mind-forged manacles
That control us one and all.

It would seem strange to us today,
This double standard against the grain,
But see it in the context of History
Even though bartering of humankind
Is still the plan of authority today.

Across the pond, in America,
When enslaved people became classed as free,
They still could not vote, go to school,
Or in a Court House give testimony, even
As late as the mid 19th Century.

In Britain the Act of Parliament of 1833
Made enslavement unlawful
After the death of the abolitionist MP

Now buried in Westminster Abbey
Alongside the Prime Minister of his day.
Strange to our enlightened minds
To read that our good and honourable friend,
Forbade his daughter's marriage to a man
Who kept enslaved people.

But to this day sugar is the sap
To the masses, consumed in quantities,
As we prate of Fairtrade hoping at least
To forget the misery, shame and horror,
Of where it's sourced and how it's grown.

While tobacco is another legal drug
Flooding the market and killing
Everything in its path.

Does the consumer pause to think?
Coffee has become another weed
Consumed in tons, with thoughtless
Lack of care but to ordinary folk,
It just happens to be there.

The European market is just the start
Portion distortion strikes the heart
While the caring health care staff

Carry the can and it just goes on.

Part Two.   Seeds of Change

A crest was painted on the ceiling
To celebrate the birth of a son.
A fine young man who went to grammar school
Then attended Cambridge University
Alongside another, a Prime Minister to be.

Representing his home town then
The whole of the locality
Leading the movement of abolition
Speaking in Parliament, a man with a Mission.

We read in our books on this moment
Of dark, dreadful history that many
Were influenced by a shift in Christianity.
It's said that the movement to evangelism
Away from more orthodox worshiping
Could have been the driving force
Behind the movement for change.

Lets not forget, however, that many
A fine, outspoken MP, were highly thought of

While perpetuating this terror of atrocity.

We know that our very own Bath newspaper
Is over two hundred and fifty years old
But they had no television, no radio
And definitely no Internet
To broadcast the change even to
The Aristocracy.

It's sobering to ponder then today
How did they ensure the Slavery Abolition Act
Was enforced? It must have taken
A bill to send to Customs and Excise
To capture at the Ports, any that offend.

Perhaps we could learn from our ancestors
In authority of those days
Because it sounds just as inhumane
To barter with people or house them
In temporary domiciles, lost in a
Sea of crippling red tape.

To put those long gone times, a very different age,
Into a perspective that we can assuage,
It was all before the dawn of electricity

But gas from burning coal became the smoky norm
For street lights lining Westminster Bridge
In that wonderful old style now revered
By followers of C.S. Lewis!

Plate 3. An old Victorian lamp post, now with an electric light bulb, outside the York Museum and next to a ruined, Priory Church, York, UK.

To put the age we tell about
In the context of its day,
Here's a man's costume, a fashion plate,
Showing a full dress coat,
A waistcoat, breeches and black, leather shoes
With ruffles of lace at wrist and chin.

Wigs were worn extensively plus
A tricorn hat as headgear was acceptable and usual.
This is the style a man would have worn
Around the time our right honourable friend
For Hull, then Yorkshire, was born.

The next image shows the fashion for women
Who would have worn a boned corset and hoops
For their crinoline, with muslin at the neck
With shoes of embroidered silk.

Plate 4. The fashion for men in the latter half of the 18th Century.

Plate 5. The fashion for women with the hoop under the skirt and the tight fitting waist, 1700s.

By the 19th Century men's fashion
Looked more sombre in colour,
The knee length breeches had been replaced
With tight pantaloons and top boots
To replace the leather shoes.

This is the introduction of the top hat and tails
Which we still see today at formal weddings
As well as the man with his old fashioned cane
Who walks before the hearse
At some funerals.

The lace we saw at a man's wrists and neckline
With all the elaborate embroidery
Has been replaced with a flowing cravat
Topping a fine, linen shirt but wool
Was the yarn for the good, broadcloth coat.

Ladies fashion was now quite different
Cotton muslin gowns with a high waist
Directly under the bust line,
Replaced the hooped skirts of their ancestors
That were woven from wool or silk.

Plate 6. A fashionable lady of the early 19th Century with long gloves and a trimmed, muslin bonnet.

It shows a change to much lighter wear
That must have been less heavy
To stand up in and carry off with flair.

At the time that Members of the British Parliament
Were arguing the case put forward
By the abolitionists, War against
Emperor Napoleon raged across the Crimea,
Europe and the Peninsula.

It made travel to Europe restricted and unsafe
So just like today, staycations were the rage.

But as our trusty and right honourable friend
Lay sick and reached his well earned rest,
Two pioneers at similar times
Discovered photography to leave an image,
That could reproduce a scene
And one of those men reported his findings
Of the negative/positive method
That was in use for a Century and a half
Until the world went digital
Before the age of computers
As this pioneer used a camera Lucida.

Plate 7. A man's attire in the UK at the turn of the 19th Century at the time of the abolitionist movement.

During the life of our honourable MP,
Railways were invented, making history.
A steam locomotive ran its race
From Stockton to Darlington at a stately pace.
In front of the engine for all to see
A man with a flag walked solemnly
While onlookers cheered its gritty progress
As passengers filled the bumpy coaches.
A cargo was also hods of coal and
Later these trains would carry stone,
Competing for speed with Canals alongside
Now these latter are restored for a pleasanter ride.

Two hundred years have elapsed since that day
Stephenson's Rocket started a new way
A revolution in transport for people and goods
Crossing the country more swiftly than before
When coaches or horseback or boats were the norm.

Later as railways crossed the land
A ride from Bath to London was planned,
Taking three hours instead of three days
A straight, level line over embankments and ways.

Plate 8. The early steam locomotive that made history by travelling from Stockton to Darlington, paving the way for rail travel that superseded stage coaches and horses.

Part Three.   Thank you, Mr Speaker.

To be a fly on the wall
At a Parliamentary debate
Would send adrenaline soaring
As men fought verbally with passion
All day and into the night.

Abolitionists vied with traditionalists
As the very status quo must change,
An inhuman, long held practice
Thought must be reframed.

An arduous battle across those famous seats
Under the eye of The Speaker
Who always sees fair play.

Order, order he would cry
Then our essential humanity
Finally won the day,
An end to decades of campaigning
Slavery Abolition Act was allowed through.

A battle indeed because once it passed in Commons,
It must be heard in Lords

While our MP for Yorkshire
Was poorly, frail but heard,
Heard that it was to be a Law
Throughout the whole British Empire.

An influence never to be underestimated
A start of a long, weary road
To speak to any who would listen
That the rights of all humankind
Must forever be upheld.

An end to traffic in enslaved people then
But for many, just the start
Of a life long, centuries struggle.

Without the need, or any necessity,
For overstatement by a mere Poet like me,
It is without doubt the responsibility
Of each and everyone to stand
United with a common bond
To stand and be counted,
To listen to the voice of the minority
To speak for the voiceless,
To hear the story of every human being
Everywhere, let the message ring out
Throughout the whole world,

Across the Globe on land or sea.

For governments speak so movingly
A deal of rhetoric, hot air, and freely,
About our rights which upheld must be
To live in perfect harmony.

Yet does this same philosophy
Translate to our daily lives?
Do we show the same concern
In everything we do, and everything
Our children learn?

Is all this fine and noble preaching,
Born out by the harsh reality of living?
For even in England in the 21st Century
Stigma is the lot of many.

But some comfort must be achieved
From the will that we hope will be redeemed
In evolving Law such that the rights of all
Can for ever be upheld.

I would love to see a day
When stigma had all dissolved away
As we continue in this constant fight

Just to share a basic right.

A song I heard has this refrain:
That change will come, but here's a thing,
I've lived in Bath, a provincial city
And seen some changes since my time
That started in 1989.

The brass band entertains us on summer Sundays
Now has women as well as men,
Soloists but still a predominance of white faces,
But in the Bank just a short distance away,
A very professional, black lady advising
In answer to my query.

Perhaps in London, Birmingham, Cardiff,
Or Bristol City it would not be noted as a
Cause celebre but how empowering
And not to be ignored.

Plate 9. The Houses of Parliament, showing the Victoria Tower, London, UK.

Plate 10. The Statue of Emmeline Pankhurst, tireless campaigner for Women's Votes, London, UK.

Part Four.   Vision and More.

It's easy to talk of human rights
From the comfort of my chair,
In the hope of broad daylight
Or when enjoying sweet fresh air.

In the spirit of democracy
Which touches our modern age,
A far cry from the battle
Made by those enslaved.

For as recently as just
The last Century, a campaign commenced
With a Bristol Bus Company.
They would not employ
Black drivers or conductors
But after a boycott, began to learn conformity.

Across the Pond, male speakers empowered
To look ahead to a life where all are free
From prejudice, judgement or bigotry.

Our own suffragettes fought for women's rights,
A creed that was once more taken
To the gates of the Houses of Parliament

Where women at last could represent
Their own constituents, the first lady MP
Just at the beginning of the last Century.

Yes it's warm and dry indoors today
While the autumn rains are pouring,
A far cry in quiet from the struggle each morning
To rise at daybreak, then pick the cotton
In the broiling sun for hours at a time,
With blisters and abrasions, no choice allowed.

Fair trade attempts to put right this wrong,
Workers are free but has it all gone?
While life remains for many a trial
For the victims of stigma, the battles go on.

Conditions aboard a slave ship
Were reported to be abominable,
With peoples crammed together and
Segregation of men from women,
In the stuffy, airless hold.
Diseases spread like wildfire
As anyone can recall
If you ever went on a coach trip
With a carrier of the common cold.

But in those days it was Dysentery
With nowhere for germs to go,
A long, slow, unbearable voyage
With an ending of greater hell.

Our caring, trusty MP for Hull
Must have been an opportunist
Because he was born sometime after
The death of another, almost as famous
And a slave owning son.

After representing the whole of Yorkshire,
The right honourable friend retired
But he was by then aged at seventy
With failing health although he lived to hear he'd won.

Once more placing all these events
In the context of historical facts and dates,
Just one month and twenty days before
The right honourable friend for Hull
Achieved his seventeenth birthday,
The American Independence Day was declared
On that special day, July fourth.

George III was on the throne of the whole

Of the United Kingdom but our MP in fact
Lived to see three kings in succession –
That's George IV next then William IV.

Part Five.   A Continued Fight

A new age of steam had dawned
As the 19th Century formed,
Steam driven ships were made of iron
But of course the Pioneers
Of transatlantic flight were operating
A Century later in bi planes designed
By the Brothers Wright.

As time moved on, the petrol engine
Gave rise to the motorcar then the omnibus was born.

It must have made a huge transition
Not seen in ages before
A massive movement of people
Who now, long haul flights enjoy.

Yes the world is a global village
As goods and services are transformed
While Britain turns full circle

Wishing to be self sufficient once more.
A sensitive issue
Right up to the present day,
As the statue of a former
Plantation owner, was toppled
Into the Bristol Harbour Bay.

It's been fished out, it's on its back,
Lying in a corner of a Museum
That commemorates all that's light and shade
Of Bristol street life up to the present day.

Fitting perhaps, as the Collegiate School
This one father founded, is thriving still
With girls now made welcome.

We hope that Modern life today
Is far more inclusive, but that's to say
That work goes on to support
The rights of all while being ever mindful
Of the need to celebrate diversity.

We acknowledge the past
Those wrongs we have made,
We continue to strive
For fruitful and positive change,

Fine words to many a wounded soul
But it's the duty of each and everyone.

Not to say it's all the government
But we have a part
So let's respond to the call
To make a start.

HOME LOVING RHYMES

AUTUMN GUSTS

Fox Hill is recently
Windier than ever before!
While I watch, a European Hornbeam
Thrashes its leaves, its branches,
In waves reminiscent of a tidal shore.

Just in front of my window
A hedge looks fit to fall,
Its evergreen foliage waves and bows
But its foundation looks shaky
With the aftermath of pruning
From the bottom, such that
It has a top heavy canopy
Rendered vulnerable to extreme.

Showers persistently blow horizontally
While the sound of distant thunder
Leads me to imagine a rumble of War.

No reassurances, the news has gone quiet,
Euthanasia rears its ugly head,
More murders, more harsh comments

While social media is buzzing
With an energy solution, nothing new there.

Yes the nuclear age is re-dawning
No one heard our prayer
Playing for political point scoring
While praising themselves all the more.

ALL SOULS

Seasonal fruit, the Pumpkin
Fills all boxes here,
Carved faces grimace
While now is the time
To light a candle for a loved one
No longer with us or here.

Nights are longer, dawn is delayed
While hope is all but lost,
Raw weather, damp mists, sharp frosts.
Stark reminder of man's engineering
Our viaduct looks over the river
As the canal hosts bright boats steering.

My breath shows misty
On the chilly air
As Advent heralds the new church year
While our hope is our Messiah
To lead us from fear,
When dawn at last emerges
From the long, dark night at the mere.

THE THIRD PROGRAM

What a ghastly, hell born racket
Tortured, twisted, tormented violin
Screaming morbid pains within!

Mother said, how wise was she,
There's always the off switch
But suddenly a turn to better harmony.

I wonder why such abject misery
Gets a massive applause not heard
For greats from the golden age!

SWARMS

Autumn, mild, dry, with berries ripening
Sees swarms of tiny gnats at my window, hearkening
Hundreds clustered by the glass
Then disappearing just as fast.

Only a few now remain
But just as quickly they will return
While an opportunistic wasp
Comes along to munch and feast.

Winging in the morning sunshine,
Sure enough, yes here they come
Seeming to increase in number
While flitting, flying, now they're gone.

BEHIND THE SCENES

Famous for its warm, reviving springs
Water for bathing, sipping, heating
Beautiful, Palladian architecture
Seats of wisdom and learning.

All of these things a tourist knows
While residents keep their secrets close
Bath is just as highly renowned
For a fixation with recycling
Everything from batteries to clothes!

Wash all rubbish before binning,
Plastics, glass, card, paper, hedge trimmings
Separating as you go, using
Seagull proof bags and caddies of course.

My mind hearkens back
To a visit I made, to South Padre Island
Across the Pond, where at an exhibition
And visitors centre, a whole heap of trash
From the Ocean was found,
Put in the shape of the human form
With a manikin's arm to set off the whole.

A stark message printed
Rang out bold to see
Of the fate of humankind
Buried alive in its own trash
As we hear commonly.

So workers set out, with tongs held aloft
To walk the canal, picking up trash
More packing, more cans
It seems as if more is always produced
An everlasting cycle, with no grounds for hope.

Allegedly the bottles we fling
Into this amazing, red bin
Are turned into fleeces
Or aeroplane seating.

But why Lady Mayor, I really must ask
Are the seats of the buses
Made of leather not grass?

I make every effort to re-use all this glass
Washing my plastic and using that bin
But it's all been negated by another's sin.

Plate 11. The big red bin for recycling plastic bottles in the City Centre of Bath UK. Its message highlights the plight of our oceans and rivers strangled by micro plastics.

STRANGE BUT TRUE

I well remember, back in the day,
Using a tuppence to phone a long way.

The pips would sound, the coin pressed in
Then they had this amazing thing:-

A book as thick as an average Thesis
With all of our numbers and all our addresses!

Technology moved a little bit forward
The phone took pound coins as notes were discontinued.

It was a long walk from home
All out in the rain

But we're all fools for love, so I bet
You did exactly the same.

Now the phone rings at the end of my arm
It's in my back pocket, it's lost all its charm.

Signature red boxes are filled now with grass
Or made into book stalls, well whatever next?

Plate 12. A signature red phone box filled with flowering plants underneath a paper canopy to resemble the rivers, Bath UK.

SUNDAY LUNCH

My tweeting buddy took
A pilgrimage to Malmesbury
Where St Athelstan has his tomb.

I took the train to Chippenham
Pausing for a lunch of sarnies, crisps and tea
But no bus on a Sunday.

I paused to snap this image
Of the age old Market Square
Where a lady was quietly reading
But of what I could not say.

The peace of God apparent
Just filled a perfect spot
I silenced a friendly scoffer
Who said, Chippenham, so what?

Perhaps next year I'll go
To see the famous tomb
But after a while another church
Is just one more pall of gloom.

Plate 12. Chippenham, Wiltshire UK, the market place with covered hen market.

CAVALCADE

Modern York has at its heart
A vast, huge railway station
The Museum houses greats of steam
Surpassed by modern electrification.

Just as I arrived by bus,
I sought my accommodation
Just to my left, the City's finest gate
With its walk on the walls
Giving the finest views
Of the Minster, up a narrow stair
Where generations had been before.

The most important gate to York
Where kings and heads of state
Bore arms to subdue the men of the North
Bearing heads upon those spikes.

Men on horseback, ladies too
Bedecked in jewels, silks of every hue,
Onlookers jostled, crowds jeered
The cavalcade passed, order restored.

But now it's just a taxi collecting fares,

Pizza delivery on motorbikes
While the stone stays weathered
But good I am sure, for another
One thousand years.

Plate 13. The old gate into the City of York, Yorkshire, UK. There is more than one gate by the city walls but this one was the most important.

CARDIFF CASTLE

Preserved for ever, loved by all
A stone carved creature, on Cardiff's wall

These are hyenas, but anteaters too
Pelicans also in a sculptured zoo.

Should you pay to step inside,
The wonder of real Welsh gold quite hides

All of the oak beams in perfect glaze
Then tiles in the nursery meet our gaze.

The banqueting hall magnificent there
For weddings, grand occasions,
But do climb the stairs –

Your ascent will be rewarded by the sight
Of the lovely roof garden, under the light.

You may not return again this year
But do it once at least if you care,

For here is a perfect piece of Welsh history

While the statue of the Marquis adorns the Square.
Plate 14. The Hyenas carved on Cardiff Castle's Boundary walls. UK.

UNCONSCIOUS GRACE

A heron pauses to feast for a fish
It must know I'm there, no movement it makes

Poised by the side of the local canal
Not worried by humans, my phone or my arm.

Just near this beautiful spot
The herons had nested, upstream there are swans

So healing a sight amidst all the grime
Not far from the City, this moment of time

An antidote here to news full of fear
This heron is only concerned with what's near

But while I was watching he kept his stance
So I didn't see his dive, or disturb his patience

Perhaps I pondered as I went on my way
Of the kind volunteers who preserve for today

The health of the water, the plants so we may
Have sights such as this heron now and always.

Plate 15. A heron watching the water of my local canal, Kennet and Avon, UK.

ST. SWITHIN'S

Legend has it that if it rains
Upon this saint's feast day
Then rain will continue for another
Forty days before the sun is restored.

This is the church, Bathonians say,
That saw the marriage of a good MP
To Barbara Spooner just before the turn
Of the nineteenth century.

Six children were their fruitful joy
And the Bishop of Oxford was a son in employ
Of the Church, but disagreed with
All of Charles Darwin and his modern creed.

While a daughter was sent to Bath
Then she espoused Reverend J James
Or so it's said.

Remembering that ladies had little say
Although they controlled the household
In a special way.

If you step inside this church

It's all in white with Georgian girth
It has a wonderful gallery
With a gilded railing where we sang
Bruckner's anthems, Bouree for Bach
Good acoustic for those melodies.

This lovely building is just across
From Hedgemead Park, another space
In a city full of green
With honeyed stone that's ever seen.

Plate 16. St. Swithin's Church, Walcot Street, Bath UK.

YORK MINSTER

A mighty cathedral with one East window
The size of a tennis court

But in a sense what's even more important
Is the warmth of its welcome

From greeters on the door
To the wonderful people who make the floral
Displays so amazing and so well thought.

Stonemasons still keep this craft alive
As conservation keeps on to today

Preserving our heritage for generations to come
With the ritual retained, traditions maintained.

At the North Transept, a window of rose
High up, overlooking the seats facing South

While in the choir stalls, the Cathedra is grand
Where the Archbishop sits formally

As the curate hands over the keys
Every long held way never falters.

Plate 17. The amazing West Front of York Minster, Seat of the Archbishop of York, UK.

PERSPECTIVE

In the foreground, it's the here and now
But far away in the remote distance
Are two figures that retreat
Like a past never seen again.

A cyclist has just sped forward
Like a future that draws ever near
Hurtling along oblivious
Of all this beauty that I survey.

Green on my left, gold on my right
Then touching my shoulder
I admire the shape of leaves
As well as the colour so bright.

A walk in the sunshine
Puts self importance to shame
In the grand scheme of things
It's washed by the autumn rains.

While here on a friendly seat, two men so good
and true, celebrated by a plaque
For serving the committee that saw our mines
filled

As our safety is now assured.
Plate 18. Part of Scholars Way, Combe Down, Bath UK.

TORTURED

In total relaxed mode I spied
A dog owner in the park.

He was hurling a ball for the Pooch
But kept tormenting the poor beast.

I watched as finally, after much hesitation
The ball was thrown to the dog's elation

A red brown spaniel rolled in the grass
While I merely wondered what else was amiss?

For after all, if the man meant to throw the ball
Why not just get on, instead of all this carry on?

But he seemed lost in his own deep thought
Unaware of my presence just like his dog

Then I kept walking and went on my way
But I think that poor dog had enough
For one day.

Plate 19. The Firs, Combe Down, Bath UK with the bench for men of the mines forum.

ARTISNAL

A macro shot of a golden leaf
Shows veins of phloem
Which to the very tips reach
Providing food from the soil below
Throughout the tree as the plant grows.

Caught in a snapshot before they fall
Their cousins still green, young and small
Strong to withstand all gales in the woods
For nearby a sapling has snapped and is dead.

Its a pleasure, a solace, a mindful delight
To view this cathedral in shades built by God
For soon the branches will be quite bare to see
As winter advances with gusts on the breeze.

A moment that never returns on this day
For drizzle descends, so I go home the same way
But the image remains impressed on my mind
Such a calming, soothing way to unwind.

Plate 20. A macro shot of golden, autumn leaves taken at Scholars Way, Combe Down, Bath UK.

JUST ONE DAY

Snow fell on one day only
A pretty, chilly moment in
March, followed by rain
For the rest of the year.

I had no plans to go out
On the road, just a few snaps
To capture this sudden
Thick, almost explosion of
No sound.

Birdsong fell silent too,
No dog barked, just the slosh
Of some quiet cars
Slowing to reach their dwellings
It was a dramatic effect.

Sages have warned that seasons have gone,
That wet follows dry instead
While today it's so mild
For late October I may see their point
As clouds bank up for yet more wet
After six months of dry but
It's not the same in the city

For my childhood was semi-rural
So there are many imponderables
But we still have leaf fall
Unlike Texas where the trees are live
Or evergreen.

It never feels like an exact science
A study of earth's heating up
But maybe the role of humankind
Is preventative whereas all we do
Is knock the symptoms on the head.

Plate 21. My neighbourhood under snow, March 2024 Bath UK

FOR MALMESBURY ABBEY (our cousin in Wiltshire)

Such a beautiful sight to see
These ancient Norman Arches
All perfect bows, topped by windows of perpendicular
With their broken reminder of fragile humanity.

I was here on Remembrance day
A busy cafe, a helpful bus driver
Lovely colours on the way
Through the countryside, a charming town.

Also a visit to the Art Gallery
Where wonderful landscapes in acrylic were
A delight to the eyes in modernist mode
How special to share with a local of that abode.

But in the Abbey four Gospels were found
Written by monks and centuries old,
Illuminated showing such patience with care
For here were believers of so long ago.
Then I found on the Northern side
The tomb of St Athelstan, but they're
Not sure where he lies.

Plate 22. Malmesbury Abbey, South side, Wiltshire, UK.

www.ingramcontent.com/pod-product-compliance
Lightning Source LLC
Chambersburg PA
CBHW052115070526
44584CB00017B/2499